The Lives of the Twelve Caesars

T. Flavius Vespasianus Augustus.
Titus Flavius Vespasianus Augustus.
Titus Flavius Domitianus.

The Lives of the Twelve Caesars

Caesars

T. Flavius Vespasianus Augustus.

Titus Flavius Vespasianus Augustus.

Titus Flavius Domitianus.

by G. Suetonius Tranquillus

©2011 SMK Books

Wilder Publications, LLC.
PO Box 3005
Radford VA 24143-3005

ISBN 10: 1-61720-579-6
ISBN 13: 978-1-61720-579-8

Table of Contents:

T. Flavius Vespasianus Augustus.

I. The empire, which had been long thrown into a disturbed and unsetted state, by the rebellion and violent death of its three last rulers, was at length restored to peace and security by the Flavian family, whose descent was indeed obscure, and which boasted no ancestral honours; but the public had no cause to regret its elevation; though it is acknowledged that Domitian met with the just reward of his avarice and cruelty. Titus Flavius Petro, a townsman of Reate , whether a centurion or an evocatus of Pompey's party in the civil war, is uncertain, fled out of the battle of Pharsalia and went home; where, having at last obtained his pardon and discharge, he became a collector of the money raised by public sales in the way of auction. His son, surnamed Sabinus, was never engaged in the military service, though some say he was a centurion of the first order, and others, that whilst he held that rank, he was discharged on account of his bad state of health: this Sabinus, I say, was a publican, and received the tax of the fortieth penny in Asia. And there were remaining, at the time of the advancement of the family, several statues, which had been erected to him by the cities of that province, with this inscription: "To the honest Tax-farmer." He afterwards turned usurer amongst the Helvetii, and there died, leaving behind him his wife, Vespasia Pella, and two sons by her; the elder of whom, Sabinus, came to be prefect of the city, and the younger, Vespasian, to be emperor. Polla, descended of a good family, at Nursia , had for her father Vespasius Pollio, thrice appointed military tribune, and at last prefect of the camp; and her brother was a senator of praetorian dignity. There is to this day, about six miles from Nursia, on the road to Spoletum, a place on the summit of a hill, called Vespasiae, where are several monuments of the Vespasii, a sufficient proof of the splendour and antiquity of the family. I will not deny that some have pretended to say, that Petro's father was a native of Gallia Transpadana , whose employment was to hire workpeople who used to emigrate every year from the country of the Umbria into that of the Sabines, to assist them in their husbandry ; but who settled at last in the town of Reate, and there married. But of this I have not been able to discover the least proof, upon the strictest inquiry.

II. Vespasian was born in the country of the Sabines, beyond Reate, in a little country-seat called Phalacrine, upon the fifth of the calends of December [27th November], in the evening, in the consulship of Quintus Sulpicius Camerinus and Caius Poppaeus Sabinus, five years before the death of

Augustus ; and was educated under the care of Tertulla, his grandmother by
the father's side, upon an estate belonging to the family, at Cosa . After his
advancement to the empire, he used frequently to visit the place where he had
spent his infancy; and the villa was continued in the same condition, that he
might see every thing about him just as he had been used to do. And he had
so great a regard for the memory of his grandmother, that, upon solemn
occasions and festival days, he constantly drank out of a silver cup which she
had been accustomed to use. After assuming the manly habit, he had a long
time a distaste for the senatorian toga, though his brother had obtained it; nor
could he be persuaded by any one but his mother to sue for that badge of
honour. She at length drove him to it, more by taunts and reproaches, than
by her entreaties and authority, calling him now and then, by way of reproach,
his brother's footman. He served as military tribune in Thrace. When made
quaestor, the province of Crete and Cyrene fell to him by lot. He was
candidate for the aedileship, and soon after for the praetorship, but met with
a repulse in the former case; though at last, with much difficulty, he came in
sixth on the poll-books. But the office of praetor he carried upon his first
canvass, standing amongst the highest at the poll. Being incensed against the
senate, and desirous to gain, by all possible means, the good graces of Caius
, he obtained leave to exhibit extraordinary games for the emperor's victory
in Germany, and advised them to increase the punishment of the conspirators
against his life, by exposing their corpses unburied. He likewise gave him
thanks in that august assembly for the honour of being admitted to his table.

III. Meanwhile, he married Flavia Domitilla, who had formerly been the
mistress of Statilius Capella, a Roman knight of Sabrata in Africa, who
enjoyed Latin rights; and was soon after declared fully and freely a citizen of
Rome, on a trial before the court of Recovery, brought by her father Flavius
Liberalis, a native of Ferentum, but no more than secretary to a quaestor. By
her he had the following children: Titus, Domitian, and Domitilla. He
outlived his wife and daughter, and lost them both before he became emperor.
After the death of his wife, he renewed his union with his former concubine
Caenis, the freedwoman of Antonia, and also her amanuensis, and treated her,
even after he was emperor, almost as if she had been his lawful wife.

IV. In the reign of Claudius, by the interest of Narcissus, he was sent to
Germany, in command of a legion; whence being removed into Britain, he
engaged the enemy in thirty several battles. He reduced under subjection to
the Romans two very powerful tribes, and above twenty great towns, with the
Isle of Wight, which lies close to the coast of Britain; partly under the

command of Aulus Plautius, the consular lieutenant, and partly under Claudius himself . For this success he received the triumphal ornaments, and in a short time after two priesthoods, besides the consulship, which he held during the two last months of the year . The interval between that and his proconsulship he spent in leisure and retirement, for fear of Agrippina, who still held great sway over her son, and hated all the friends of Narcissus, who was then dead. Afterwards he got by lot the province of Africa, which he governed with great reputation, excepting that once, in an insurrection at Adrumetum, he was pelted with turnips. It is certain that he returned thence nothing richer; for his credit was so low, that he was obliged to mortgage his whole property to his brother, and was reduced to the necessity of dealing in mules, for the support of his rank; for which reason he was commonly called "the Muleteer." He is said likewise to have been convicted of extorting from a young man of fashion two hundred thousand sesterces for procuring him the broad-stripe, contrary to the wishes of his father, and was severely reprimanded for it. While in attendance upon Nero in Achaia, he frequently withdrew from the theatre while Nero was singing, and went to sleep if he remained, which gave so much offence, that he was not only excluded from his society, but debarred the liberty of saluting him in public. Upon this, he retired to a small out-of-the-way town, where he lay skulking in constant fear of his life, until a province, with an army, was offered him.

A firm persuasion had long prevailed through all the East , that it was fated for the empire of the world, at that time, to devolve on some who should go forth from Judaea. This prediction referred to a Roman emperor, as the event shewed; but the Jews, applying it to themselves, broke out into rebellion, and having defeated and slain their governor , routed the lieutenant of Syria , a man of consular rank, who was advancing to his assistance, and took an eagle, the standard, of one of his legions. As the suppression of this revolt appeared to require a stronger force and an active general, who might be safely trusted in an affair of so much importance, Vespasian was chosen in preference to all others, both for his known activity, and on account of the obscurity of his origin and name, being a person of whom there could be not the least jealousy. Two legions, therefore, eight squadrons of horse, and ten cohorts, being added to the former troops in Judaea, and, taking with him his eldest son as lieutenant, as soon as he arrived in his province, he turned the eyes of the neighbouring provinces upon him, by reforming immediately the discipline of the camp, and engaging the enemy once or twice with such resolution, that, in the attack of a castle , he had his knee hurt by the stroke of a stone, and received several arrows in his shield.

V. After the deaths of Nero and Galba, whilst Otho and Vitellius were contending for the sovereignty, he entertained hopes of obtaining the empire, with the prospect of which he had long before flattered himself, from the following omens. Upon an estate belonging to the Flavian family, in the neighbourhood of Rome, there was an old oak, sacred to Mars, which, at the three several deliveries of Vespasia, put out each time a new branch; evident intimations of the future fortune of each child. The first was but a slender one, which quickly withered away; and accordingly, the girl that was born did not live long. The second became vigorous, which portended great good fortune; but the third grew like a tree. His father, Sabinus, encouraged by these omens, which were confirmed by the augurs, told his mother, "that her grandson would be emperor of Rome;" at which she laughed heartily, wondering, she said, "that her son should be in his dotage whilst she continued still in full possession of her faculties."

Afterwards in his aedileship, when Caius Caesar, being enraged at his not taking care to have the streets kept clean, ordered the soldiers to fill the bosom of his gown with dirt, some persons at that time construed it into a sign that the government, being trampled under foot and deserted in some civil commotion, would fall under his protection, and as it were into his lap. Once, while he was at dinner, a strange dog, that wandered about the streets, brought a man's hand , and laid it under the table. And another time, while he was at supper, a plough-ox throwing the yoke off his neck, broke into the room, and after he had frightened away all the attendants, on a sudden, as if he was tired, fell down at his feet, as he lay still upon his couch, and hung down his neck. A cypress-tree likewise, in a field belonging to the family, was torn up by the roots, and laid flat upon the ground, when there was no violent wind; but next day it rose again fresher and stronger than before.

He dreamt in Achaia that the good fortune of himself and his family would begin when Nero had a tooth drawn; and it happened that the day after, a surgeon coming into the hall, showed him a tooth which he had just extracted from Nero. In Judaea, upon his consulting the oracle of the divinity at Carmel , the answer was so encouraging as to assure him of success in anything he projected, however great or important it might be. And when Josephus , one of the noble prisoners, was put in chains, he confidently affirmed that he should be released in a very short time by the same Vespasian, but he would be emperor first . Some omens were likewise mentioned in the news from

Rome, and among others, that Nero, towards the close of his days, was commanded in a dream to carry Jupiter's sacred chariot out of the sanctuary where it stood, to Vespasian's house, and conduct it thence into the circus. Also not long afterwards, as Galba was going to the election, in which he was created consul for the second time, a statue of the Divine Julius   turned towards the east. And in the field of Bedriacum , before the battle began, two eagles engaged in the sight of the army; and one of them being beaten, a third came from the east, and drove away the conqueror.

VI. He made, however, no attempt upon the sovereignty, though his friends were very ready to support him, and even pressed him to the enterprise, until he was encouraged to it by the fortuitous aid of persons unknown to him and at a distance. Two thousand men, drawn out of three legions in the Moesian army, had been sent to the assistance of Otho. While they were upon their march, news came that he had been defeated, and had put an end to his life; notwithstanding which they continued their march as far as Aquileia, pretending that they gave no credit to the report. There, tempted by the opportunity which the disorder of the times afforded them, they ravaged and plundered the country at discretion; until at length, fearing to be called to an account on their return, and punished for it, they resolved upon choosing and creating an emperor. "For they were no ways inferior," they said, "to the army which made Galba emperor, nor to the pretorian troops which had set up Otho, nor the army in Germany, to whom Vitellius owed his elevation." The names of all the consular lieutenants, therefore, being taken into consideration, and one objecting to one, and another to another, for various reasons; at last some of the third legion, which a little before Nero's death had been removed out of Syria into Moesia, extolled Vespasian in high terms; and all the rest assenting, his name was immediately inscribed on their standards. The design was nevertheless quashed for a time, the troops being brought to submit to Vitellius a little longer.

However, the fact becoming known, Tiberius Alexander, governor of Egypt, first obliged the legions under his command to swear obedience to Vespasian as their emperor, on the calends [the 1st] of July, which was observed ever after as the day of his accession to the empire; and upon the fifth of the ides of the same month [the 28th July], the army in Judaea, where he then was, also swore allegiance to him. What contributed greatly to forward the affair, was a copy of a letter, whether real or counterfeit, which was circulated, and said to have been written by Otho before his decease to Vespasian, recommending to him in the most urgent terms to avenge his death, and entreating him to come to the aid of the commonwealth; as well as a report which was circulated, that Vitellius, after his success against Otho, proposed to change the winter quarters of the legions, and remove those in Germany to a less hazardous station and a warmer climate. Moreover, amongst the governors of provinces, Licinius Mucianus dropping the grudge arising from a jealousy of which he had hitherto made no secret, promised to join him with the Syrian army, and, among the allied kings, Volugesus, king of the Parthians, offered him a reinforcement of forty thousand archers.

VII. Having, therefore, entered on a civil war, and sent forward his generals and forces into Italy, he himself, in the meantime, passed over to Alexandria, to obtain possession of the key of Egypt . Here having entered alone, without attendants, the temple of Serapis, to take the auspices respecting the establishment of his power, and having done his utmost to propitiate the deity, upon turning round, [his freedman] Basilides appeared before him, and seemed to offer him the sacred leaves, chaplets, and cakes, according to the usage of the place, although no one had admitted him, and he had long laboured under a muscular debility, which would hardly have allowed him to walk into the temple; besides which, it was certain that at the very time he was far away. Immediately after this, arrived letters with intelligence that Vitellius's troops had been defeated at Cremona, and he himself slain at Rome. Vespasian, the new emperor, having been raised unexpectedly from a low estate, wanted something which might clothe him with divine majesty and authority. This, likewise, was now added. A poor man who was blind, and another who was lame, came both together before him, when he was seated on the tribunal, imploring him to heal them , and saying that they were admonished in a dream by the god Serapis to seek his aid, who assured them that he would restore sight to the one by anointing his eyes with his spittle, and give strength to the leg of the other, if he vouchsafed but to touch it with his heel. At first he could scarcely believe that the thing would any how succeed, and therefore hesitated to venture on making the experiment. At length, however, by the advice of his friends, he made the attempt publicly, in the presence of the assembled multitudes, and it was crowned with success in both cases . About the same time, at Tegea in Arcadia, by the direction of some soothsayers, several vessels of ancient workmanship were dug out of a consecrated place, on which there was an effigy resembling Vespasian.

VIII. Returning now to Rome, under these auspices, and with a great reputation, after enjoying a triumph for victories over the Jews, he added eight consulships to his former one. He likewise assumed the censorship, and made it his principal concern, during the whole of his government, first to restore order in the state, which had been almost ruined, and was in a tottering condition, and then to improve it. The soldiers, one part of them emboldened by victory, and the other smarting with the disgrace of their defeat, had abandoned themselves to every species of licentiousness and insolence. Nay, the provinces, too, and free cities, and some kingdoms in alliance with Rome, were all in a disturbed state. He, therefore, disbanded many of Vitellius's soldiers, and punished others; and so far was he from granting any extraordinary favours to the sharers of his success, that it was late before he paid the gratuities due to them by law. That he might let slip no opportunity of reforming the discipline of the army, upon a young man's coming much perfumed to return him thanks for having appointed him to command a squadron of horse, he turned away his head in disgust, and, giving him this sharp reprimand, "I had rather you had smelt of garlic," revoked his commission. When the men belonging to the fleet, who travelled by turns from Ostia and Puteoli to Rome, petitioned for an addition to their pay, under the name of shoe-money, thinking that it would answer little purpose to send them away without a reply, he ordered them for the future to run barefooted; and so they have done ever since. He deprived of their liberties, Achaia, Lycia, Rhodes, Byzantium, and Samos; and reduced them into the form of provinces; Thrace, also, and Cilicia, as well as Comagene, which until that time had been under the government of kings. He stationed some legions in Cappadocia on account of the frequent inroads of the barbarians, and, instead of a Roman knight, appointed as governor of it a man of consular rank. The ruins of houses which had been burnt down long before, being a great desight to the city, he gave leave to any one who would, to take possession of the void ground and build upon it, if the proprietors should hesitate to perform the work themselves. He resolved upon rebuilding the Capitol, and was the foremost to put his hand to clearing the ground of the rubbish, and removed some of it upon his own shoulder. And he undertook, likewise, to restore the three thousand tables of brass which had been destroyed in the fire which consumed the Capitol; searching in all quarters for copies of those curious and ancient records, in which were contained the decrees of the senate, almost from the building of the city, as well as the acts of the people, relative to alliances, treaties, and privileges granted to any person.

IX. He likewise erected several new public buildings, namely, the temple of Peace near the Forum, that of Claudius on the Coelian mount, which had been begun by Agrippina, but almost entirely demolished by Nero ; and an amphitheatre in the middle of the city, upon finding that Augustus had projected such a work. He purified the senatorian and equestrian orders, which had been much reduced by the havoc made amongst them at several times, and was fallen into disrepute by neglect. Having expelled the most unworthy, he chose in their room the most honourable persons in Italy and the provinces. And to let it be known that those two orders differed not so much in privileges as in dignity, he declared publicly, when some altercation passed between a senator and a Roman knight, "that senators ought not to be treated with scurrilous language, unless they were the aggressors, and then it was fair and lawful to return it."

X. The business of the courts had prodigiously accumulated, partly from old law-suits which, on account of the interruption that had been given to the course of justice, still remained undecided, and partly from the accession of new suits arising out of the disorder of the times. He, therefore, chose commissioners by lot to provide for the restitution of what had been seized by violence during the war, and others with extraordinary jurisdiction to decide causes belonging to the centumviri, and reduce them to as small a number as possible, for the dispatch of which, otherwise, the lives of the litigants could scarcely allow sufficient time.

XI. Lust and luxury, from the licence which had long prevailed, had also grown to an enormous height. He, therefore, obtained a decree of the senate, that a woman who formed an union with the slave of another person, should be considered a bondwoman herself; and that usurers should not be allowed to take proceedings at law for the recovery of money lent to young men whilst they lived in their father's family, not even after their fathers were dead.

XII. In other affairs, from the beginning to the end of his government, he conducted himself with great moderation and clemency. He was so far from dissembling the obscurity of his extraction, that he frequently made mention of it himself. When some affected to trace his pedigree to the founders of Reate, and a companion of Hercules , whose monument is still to be seen on the Salarian road, he laughed at them for it. And he was so little fond of external and adventitious ornaments, that, on the day of his triumph , being quite tired of the length and tediousness of the procession, he could not forbear saying, "he was rightly served, for having in his old age been so silly as to desire a triumph; as if it was either due to his ancestors, or had ever been expected by himself." Nor would he for a long time accept of the tribunitian authority, or the title of Father of his Country. And in regard to the custom of searching those who came to salute him, he dropped it even in the time of the civil war.

XIII. He bore with great mildness the freedom used by his friends, the satirical allusions of advocates, and the petulance of philosophers. Licinius Mucianus, who had been guilty of notorious acts of lewdness, but, presuming upon his great services, treated him very rudely, he reproved only in private; and when complaining of his conduct to a common friend of theirs, he concluded with these words, "However, I am a man." Salvius Liberalis, in pleading the cause of a rich man under prosecution, presuming to say, "What is it to Caesar, if Hipparchus possesses a hundred millions of sesterces?" he commended him for it. Demetrius, the Cynic philosopher , who had been sentenced to banishment, meeting him on the road, and refusing to rise up or salute him, nay, snarling at him in scurrilous language, he only called him a cur.

XIV. He was little disposed to keep up the memory of affronts or quarrels, nor did he harbour any resentment on account of them. He made a very splendid marriage for the daughter of his enemy Vitellius, and gave her, besides, a suitable fortune and equipage. Being in a great consternation after he was forbidden the court in the time of Nero, and asking those about him, what he should do? or, whither he should go? one of those whose office it was to introduce people to the emperor, thrusting him out, bid him go to Morbonia . But when this same person came afterwards to beg his pardon, he only vented his resentment in nearly the same words. He was so far from being influenced by suspicion or fear to seek the destruction of any one, that, when his friends advised him to beware of Metius Pomposianus, because it was commonly believed, on his nativity being cast, that he was destined by fate to the empire, he made him consul, promising for him, that he would not forget the benefit conferred.

XV. It will scarcely be found, that so much as one innocent person suffered in his reign, unless in his absence, and without his knowledge, or, at least, contrary to his inclination, and when he was imposed upon. Although Helvidius Priscus was the only man who presumed to salute him on his return from Syria by his private name of Vespasian, and, when he came to be praetor, omitted any mark of honour to him, or even any mention of him in his edicts, yet he was not angry, until Helvidius proceeded to inveigh against him with the most scurrilous language. Though he did indeed banish him, and afterwards ordered him to be put to death, yet he would gladly have saved him notwithstanding, and accordingly dispatched messengers to fetch back the executioners; and he would have saved him, had he not been deceived by a false account brought, that he had already perished. He never rejoiced at the death of any man; nay he would shed tears, and sigh, at the just punishment of the guilty.

XVI. The only thing deservedly blameable in his character was his love of money. For not satisfied with reviving the imposts which had been repealed in the time of Galba, he imposed new and onerous taxes, augmented the tribute of the provinces, and doubled that of some of them. He likewise openly engaged in a traffic, which is discreditable even to a private individual, buying great quantities of goods, for the purpose of retailing them again to advantage. Nay, he made no scruple of selling the great offices of the state to candidates, and pardons to persons under prosecution, whether they were innocent or guilty. It is believed, that he advanced all the most rapacious amongst the procurators to higher offices, with the view of squeezing them after they had acquired great wealth. He was commonly said, "to have used them as sponges," because it was his practice, as we may say, to wet them when dry, and squeeze them when wet. It is said that he was naturally extremely covetous, and was upbraided with it by an old herdsman of his, who, upon the emperor's refusing to enfranchise him gratis, which on his advancement he humbly petitioned for, cried out, "That the fox changed his hair, but not his nature." On the other hand, some are of opinion, that he was urged to his rapacious proceedings by necessity, and the extreme poverty of the treasury and exchequer, of which he took public notice in the beginning of his reign; declaring that "no less than four hundred thousand millions of sesterces were wanting to carry on the government." This is the more likely to be true, because he applied to the best purposes what he procured by bad means.

XVII. His liberality, however, to all ranks of people, was excessive. He made up to several senators the estate required by law to qualify them for that dignity; relieving likewise such men of consular rank as were poor, with a yearly allowance of five hundred thousand sesterces ; and rebuilt, in a better manner than before, several cities in different parts of the empire, which had been damaged by earthquakes or fires.

XVIII. He was a great encourager of learning and the liberal arts. He first granted to the Latin and Greek professors of rhetoric the yearly stipend of a hundred thousand sesterces each out of the exchequer. He also bought the freedom of superior poets and artists , and gave a noble gratuity to the restorer of the Coan of Venus , and to another artist who repaired the Colossus . Some one offering to convey some immense columns into the Capitol at a small expense by a mechanical contrivance, he rewarded him very handsomely for his invention, but would not accept his service, saying, "Suffer me to find maintenance for the poor people."

XIX. In the games celebrated when the stage-scenery of the theatre of Marcellus was repaired, he restored the old musical entertainments. He gave Apollinaris, the tragedian, four hundred thousand sesterces, and to Terpinus and Diodorus, the harpers, two hundred thousand; to some a hundred thousand; and the least he gave to any of the performers was forty thousand, besides many golden crowns. He entertained company constantly at his table, and often in great state and very sumptuously, in order to promote trade. As in the Saturnalia he made presents to the men which they were to carry away with them, so did he to the women upon the calends of March ; notwithstanding which, he could not wipe off the disrepute of his former stinginess. The Alexandrians called him constantly Cybiosactes; a name which had been given to one of their kings who was sordidly avaricious. Nay, at his funeral, Favo, the principal mimic, personating him, and imitating, as actors do, both his manner of speaking and his gestures, asked aloud of the procurators, "how much his funeral and the procession would cost?" And being answered "ten millions of sesterces," he cried out, "give him but a hundred thousand sesterces, and they might throw his body into the Tiber, if they would."

XX. He was broad-set, strong-limbed, and his features gave the idea of a man in the act of straining himself. In consequence, one of the city wits, upon the emperor's desiring him "to say something droll respecting himself," facetiously answered, "I will, when you have done relieving your bowels." He enjoyed a good state of health, though he used no other means to preserve it, than repeated friction, as much as he could bear, on his neck and other parts of his body, in the tennis-court attached to the baths, besides fasting one day in every month.

XXI. His method of life was commonly this. After he became emperor, he used to rise very early, often before daybreak. Having read over his letters, and the briefs of all the departments of the government offices; he admitted his friends; and while they were paying him their compliments, he would put on his own shoes, and dress himself with his own hands. Then, after the dispatch of such business as was brought before him, he rode out, and afterwards retired to repose, lying on his couch with one of his mistresses, of whom he kept several after the death of Caenis . Coming out of his private apartments, he passed to the bath, and then entered the supper-room. They say that he was never more good-humoured and indulgent than at that time: and therefore his attendants always seized that opportunity, when they had any favour to ask.

XXII. At supper, and, indeed, at other times, he was extremely free and jocose. For he had humour, but of a low kind, and he would sometimes use indecent language, such as is addressed to young girls about to be married. Yet there are some things related of him not void of ingenious pleasantry; amongst which are the following. Being once reminded by Mestrius Florus, that plaustra was a more proper expression than plostra, he the next day saluted him by the name of Flaurus . A certain lady pretending to be desperately enamoured of him, he was prevailed upon to admit her to his bed; and after he had gratified her desires, he gave her four hundred thousand sesterces. When his steward desired to know how he would have the sum entered in his accounts, he replied, "For Vespasian's being seduced."

XXIII. He used Greek verses very wittily; speaking of a tall man, who had enormous parts:

Makxi bibas, kradon dolichoskion enchos;
Still shaking, as he strode, his vast long spear.

And of Cerylus, a freedman, who being very rich, had begun to pass himself off as free-born, to elude the exchequer at his decease, and assumed the name of Laches, he said:

—O Lachaes, Lachaes,
Epan apothanaes, authis ex archaes esae Kaerylos.

Ah, Laches, Laches! when thou art no more,
Thou'lt Cerylus be called, just as before.

He chiefly affected wit upon his own shameful means of raising money, in order to wipe off the odium by some joke, and turn it into ridicule. One of his ministers, who was much in his favour, requesting of him a stewardship for some person, under pretence of his being his brother, he deferred granting him his petition, and in the meantime sent for the candidate, and having squeezed out of him as much money as he had agreed to give to his friend at court, he appointed him immediately to the office. The minister soon after renewing his application, "You must," said he, "find another brother; for the one you adopted is in truth mine."

Suspecting once, during a journey, that his mule-driver had alighted to shoe his mules, only in order to have an opportunity for allowing a person they met, who was engaged in a law-suit, to speak to him, he asked him, "how much he got for shoeing his mules?" and insisted on having a share of the profit. When his son Titus blamed him for even laying a tax upon urine, he applied to his nose a piece of the money he received in the first instalment, and asked him, "if it stunk?" And he replying no, "And yet," said he, "it is derived from urine."

Some deputies having come to acquaint him that a large statue, which would cost a vast sum, was ordered to be erected for him at the public expense, he told them to pay it down immediately, holding out the hollow of his hand, and saying, "there was a base ready for the statue." Not even when he was under the immediate apprehension and peril of death, could he forbear jesting. For when, among other prodigies, the mausoleum of the Caesars suddenly flew open, and a blazing star appeared in the heavens; one of the prodigies, he said, concerned Julia Calvina, who was of the family of Augustus ; and the other, the king of the Parthians, who wore his hair long. And when his distemper first seized him, "I suppose," said he, "I shall soon be a god."

XXIV. In his ninth consulship, being seized, while in Campania, with a slight indisposition, and immediately returning to the city, he soon afterwards went thence to Cutiliae , and his estates in the country about Reate, where he used constantly to spend the summer. Here, though his disorder much increased, and he injured his bowels by too free use of the cold waters, he nevertheless attended to the dispatch of business, and even gave audience to ambassadors in bed. At last, being taken ill of a diarrhoea, to such a degree that he was ready to faint, he cried out, "An emperor ought to die standing upright." In endeavouring to rise, he died in the hands of those who were helping him up, upon the eighth of the calends of July [24th June] , being sixty-nine years, one month, and seven days old.

XXV. All are agreed that he had such confidence in the calculations on his own nativity and that of his sons, that, after several conspiracies against him, he told the senate, that either his sons would succeed him, or nobody. It is said likewise, that he once saw in a dream a balance in the middle of the porch of the Palatine house exactly poised; in one scale of which stood Claudius and Nero, in the other, himself and his sons. The event corresponded to the symbol; for the reigns of the two parties were precisely of the same duration.

Neither consanguinity nor adoption, as formerly, but great influence in the army having now become the road to the imperial throne, no person could claim a better title to that elevation than Titus Flavius Vespasian. He had not only served with great reputation in the wars both in Britain and Judaea, but seemed as yet untainted with any vice which could pervert his conduct in the civil administration of the empire. It appears, however, that he was prompted more by the persuasion of friends, than by his own ambition, to prosecute the attainment of the imperial dignity. To render this enterprise more successful, recourse was had to a new and peculiar artifice, which, while well accommodated to the superstitious credulity of the Romans, impressed them with an idea, that Vespasian's destiny to the throne was confirmed by supernatural indications. But, after his elevation, we hear no more of his miraculous achievements.

The prosecution of the war in Britain, which had been suspended for some years, was resumed by Vespasian; and he sent thither Petilius Cerealis, who by his bravery extended the limits of the Roman province. Under Julius Frontinus, successor to that general, the invaders continued to make farther progress in the reduction of the island: but the commander who finally established the dominion of the Romans in Britain, was Julius Agricola, not less distinguished for his military achievements, than for his prudent regard to the civil administration of the country. He began his operations with the conquest of North Wales, whence passing over into the island of Anglesey, which had revolted since the time of Suetonius Paulinus, he again reduced it to subjection. Then proceeding northwards with his victorious army, he defeated the Britons in every engagement, took possession of all the territories in the southern parts of the island, and driving before him all who refused to submit to the Roman arms, penetrated even into the forests and mountains of Caledonia. He defeated the natives under Galgacus, their leader, in a decisive battle; and fixing a line of garrisons between the friths of Clyde and Forth, he secured the Roman province from the incursions of the people who occupied the parts of the island beyond that boundary. Wherever he established the Roman power, he introduced laws and civilization amongst the inhabitants, and employed every means of conciliating their affection, as well as of securing their obedience.

The war in Judaea, which had been commenced under the former reign, was continued in that of Vespasian; but he left the siege of Jerusalem to be conducted by his son Titus, who displayed great valour and military talents in the prosecution of the enterprise. After an obstinate defence by the Jews, that city, so much celebrated in the sacred writings, was finally demolished, and the glorious temple itself, the admiration of the world, reduced to ashes; contrary, however, to the will of Titus, who exerted his utmost efforts to extinguish the flames.

The manners of the Romans had now attained to an enormous pitch of depravity, through the unbounded licentiousness of the tines; and, to the honour of Vespasian, he discovered great zeal in his endeavours to effect a national reformation. Vigilant, active, and persevering, he was indefatigable in the management of public affairs, and rose in the winter before day-break, to give audience to his officers of state. But if we give credit to the whimsical imposition of a tax upon urine, we cannot entertain any high opinion, either of his talents as a financier, or of the resources of the Roman empire. By his encouragement of science, he displayed a liberality, of which there occurs no example under all the preceding emperors, since the time of Augustus. Pliny the elder was now in the height of reputation, as well as in great favour with Vespasian; and it was probably owing not a little to the advice of that minister, that the emperor showed himself so much the patron of literary men. A writer mentioned frequently by Pliny, and who lived in this reign, was Licinius Mucianus, a Roman knight: he treated of the history and geography of the eastern countries. Juvenal, who had begun his Satires several years before, continued to inveigh against the flagrant vices of the times; but the only author whose writings we have to notice in the present reign, is a poet of a different class.

C. VALERIUS FLACCUS wrote a poem in eight books, on the Expedition of the Argonauts; a subject which, next to the wars of Thebes and Troy, was in ancient times the most celebrated. Of the life of this author, biographers have transmitted no particulars; but we may place his birth in the reign of Tiberius, before all the writers who flourished in the Augustan age were extinct. He enjoyed the rays of the setting sun which had illumined that glorious period, and he discovers the efforts of an ambition to recall its meridian splendour. As the poem was left incomplete by the death of the author, we can only judge imperfectly of the conduct and general consistency of the fable: but the most difficult part having been executed, without any room for the censure of candid criticism, we may presume that the sequel would have been finished with an equal claim to indulgence, if not to applause. The traditional anecdotes relative to the Argonautic expedition are introduced with propriety, and embellished with the graces of poetical fiction. In describing scenes of tenderness, this author is happily pathetic, and in the heat of combat, proportionably animated. His similes present the imagination with beautiful imagery, and not only illustrate, but give additional force to the subject. We find in Flaccus a few expressions not countenanced by the authority of the most celebrated Latin writers. His language, however, in general, is pure; but his words are perhaps not always the best that might have been chosen. The versification is elevated, though not uniformly harmonious; and there pervades the whole poem an epic dignity, which renders it superior to the production ascribed to Orpheus, or to that of Apollonius, on the same subject.

Titus Flavius Vespasianus Augustus.

I. Titus, who had the same cognomen with his father, was the darling and delight of mankind; so much did the natural genius, address, or good fortune he possessed tend to conciliate the favour of all. This was, indeed, extremely difficult, after he became emperor, as before that time, and even during the reign of his father, he lay under public odium and censure. He was born upon the third of the calends of January, [30th Dec.] in the year remarkable for the death of Caius , near the Septizonium , in a mean house, and a very small and dark room, which still exists, and is shown to the curious.

II. He was educated in the palace with Britannicus, and instructed in the same branches of learning, and under the same masters. During this time, they say, that a physiognomist being introduced by Narcissus, the freedman of Claudius, to examine the features of Britannicus , positively affirmed that he would never become emperor, but that Titus, who stood by, would. They were so familiar, that Titus being next him at table, is thought to have tasted of the fatal potion which put an end to Britannicus's life, and to have contracted from it a distemper which hung about him a long time. In remembrance of all these circumstances, he afterwards erected a golden statue of him in the Palatium, and dedicated to him an equestrian statue of ivory; attending it in the Circensian procession, in which it is still carried to this day.

III. While yet a boy, he was remarkable for his noble endowments both of body and mind; and as he advanced in years, they became still more conspicuous. He had a fine person, combining an equal mixture of majesty and grace; was very strong, though not tall, and somewhat corpulent. Gifted with an excellent memory, and a capacity for all the arts of peace and war; he was a perfect master of the use of arms and riding; very ready in the Latin and Greek tongues, both in verse and prose; and such was the facility he possessed in both, that he would harangue and versify extempore. Nor was he unacquainted with music, but could both sing and play upon the harp sweetly and scientifically. I have likewise been informed by many persons, that he was remarkably quick in writing short-hand, would in merriment and jest engage with his secretaries in the imitation of any hand-writing he saw, and often say, "that he was admirably qualified for forgery."

IV. He filled with distinction the rank of a military tribune both in Germany and Britain, in which he conducted himself with the utmost activity, and no less modesty and reputation; as appears evident from the great number of statues, with honourable inscriptions, erected to him in various parts of both those provinces. After serving in the wars, he frequented the courts of law, but with less assiduity than applause. About the same time, he married Arricidia, the daughter of Tertullus, who was only a knight, but had formerly been prefect of the pretorian guards. After her decease, he married Marcia Furnilla, of a very noble family, but afterwards divorced her, taking from her the daughter he had by her. Upon the expiration of his quaestorship, he was raised to the rank of commander of a legion , and took the two strong cities of Tarichaea and Gamala, in Judaea; and having his horse killed under him in a battle, he mounted another, whose rider he had encountered and slain.

V. Soon afterwards, when Galba came to be emperor, he was sent to congratulate him, and turned the eyes of all people upon himself, wherever he came; it being the general opinion amongst them, that the emperor had sent for him with a design to adopt him for his son. But finding all things again in confusion, he turned back upon the road; and going to consult the oracle of Venus at Paphos about his voyage, he received assurances of obtaining the empire for himself. These hopes were speedily strengthened, and being left to finish the reduction of Judaea, in the final assault of Jerusalem, he slew seven of its defenders, with the like number of arrows, and took it upon his daughter's birth-day . So great was the joy and attachment of the soldiers, that, in their congratulations, they unanimously saluted him by the title of Emperor ; and, upon his quitting the province soon afterwards, would needs have detained him, earnestly begging him, and that not without threats, "either to stay, or take them all with him." This occurrence gave rise to the suspicion of his being engaged in a design to rebel against his father, and claim for himself the government of the East; and the suspicion increased, when, on his way to Alexandria, he wore a diadem at the consecration of the ox Apis at Memphis; and, though he did it only in compliance with an ancient religious usage of the country, yet there was some who put a bad construction upon it. Making, therefore, what haste he could into Italy, he arrived first at Rhegium, and sailing thence in a merchant ship to Puteoli, went to Rome with all possible expedition. Presenting himself unexpectedly to his father, he said, by way of contradicting the strange reports raised concerning him, "I am come, father, I am come."

VI. From that time he constantly acted as colleague with his father, and, indeed, as regent of the empire. He triumphed with his father, bore jointly with him the office of censor , and was, besides, his colleague not only in the tribunitian authority , but in seven consulships . Taking upon himself the care and inspection of all offices, he dictated letters, wrote proclamations in his father's name, and pronounced his speeches in the senate in place of the quaestor. He likewise assumed the command of the pretorian guards, although no one but a Roman knight had ever before been their prefect. In this he conducted himself with great haughtiness and violence, taking off without scruple or delay all those he had most reason to suspect, after he had secretly sent his emissaries into the theatres and camp, to demand, as if by general consent, that the suspected persons should be delivered up to punishment. Among these, he invited to supper A. Caecina, a man of consular rank, whom he ordered to be stabbed at his departure, immediately after he had gone out of the room. To this act, indeed, he was provoked by an imminent danger; for he had discovered a writing under the hand of Caecina, containing an account of a plot hatched among the soldiers. By these acts, though he provided for his future security, yet for the present he so much incurred the hatred of the people, that scarcely ever any one came to the empire with a more odious character, or more universally disliked.

VII. Besides his cruelty, he lay under the suspicion of giving way to habits of luxury, as he often prolonged his revels till midnight with the most riotous of his acquaintance. Nor was he unsuspected of lewdness, on account of the swarms of catamites and eunuchs about him, and his well-known attachment to queen Berenice , who received from him, as it is reported, a promise of marriage. He was supposed, besides, to be of a rapacious disposition; for it is certain, that, in causes which came before his father, he used to offer his interest for sale, and take bribes. In short, people publicly expressed an unfavourable opinion of him, and said he would prove another Nero. This prejudice, however, turned out in the end to his advantage, and enhanced his praises to the highest pitch when he was found to possess no vicious propensities, but, on the contrary, the noblest virtues. His entertainments were agreeable rather than extravagant; and he surrounded himself with such excellent friends, that the succeeding princes adopted them as most serviceable to themselves and the state. He immediately sent away Berenice from the city, much against both their inclinations. Some of his old eunuchs, though such accomplished dancers, that they bore an uncontrollable sway upon the stage, he was so far from treating with any extraordinary kindness, that he would not so much as witness their performances in the crowded theatre. He violated no private right; and if ever man refrained from injustice, he did; nay, he would not accept of the allowable and customary offerings. Yet, in munificence, he was inferior to none of the princes before him. Having dedicated his amphitheatre , and built some warm baths close by it with great expedition, he entertained the people with most magnificent spectacles. He likewise exhibited a naval fight in the old Naumachia, besides a combat of gladiators; and in one day brought into the theatre five thousand wild beasts of all kinds.

VIII. He was by nature extremely benevolent; for whereas all the emperors after Tiberius, according to the example he had set them, would not admit the grants made by former princes to be valid, unless they received their own sanction, he confirmed them all by one general edict, without waiting for any applications respecting them. Of all who petitioned for any favour, he sent none away without hopes. And when his ministers represented to him that he promised more than he could perform, he replied, "No one ought to go away downcast from an audience with his prince." Once at supper, reflecting that he had done nothing for any that day, he broke out into that memorable and justly-admired saying, "My friends, I have lost a day." More particularly, he treated the people on all occasions with so much courtesy, that, on his presenting them with a show of gladiators, he declared, "He should manage it, not according to his own fancy, but that of the spectators," and did accordingly. He denied them nothing, and very frankly encouraged them to ask what they pleased. Espousing the cause of the Thracian party among the gladiators, he frequently joined in the popular demonstrations in their favour, but without compromising his dignity or doing injustice. To omit no opportunity of acquiring popularity, he sometimes made use himself of the baths he had erected, without excluding the common people. There happened in his reign some dreadful accidents; an eruption of Mount Vesuvius , in Campania, and a fire in Rome, which continued during three days and three nights ; besides a plague, such as was scarcely ever known before. Amidst these many great disasters, he not only manifested the concern which might be expected from a prince but even the affection of a father, for his people; one while comforting them by his proclamations, and another while relieving them to the utmost of his power. He chose by lot, from amongst the men of consular rank, commissioners for repairing the losses in Campania. The estates of those who had perished by the eruption of Vesuvius, and who had left no heirs, he applied to the repair of the ruined cities. With regard to the public buildings destroyed by fire in the City, he declared that nobody should be a loser but himself. Accordingly, he applied all the ornaments of his palaces to the decoration of the temples, and purposes of public utility, and appointed several men of the equestrian order to superintend the work. For the relief of the people during the plague, he employed, in the way of sacrifice and medicine, all means both human and divine. Amongst the calamities of the times, were informers and their agents; a tribe of miscreants who had grown up under the licence of former reigns. These he frequently ordered to be scourged or beaten with sticks in the Forum, and then, after he had obliged them to pass through the amphitheatre as a public spectacle, commanded them to be sold for slaves, or else banished them to some rocky islands. And to discourage such practices for the future, amongst other things, he prohibited actions to be successively brought under different laws for the same cause, or the state of affairs of deceased persons to be inquired into after a certain number of years.

IX. Having declared that he accepted the office of Pontifex Maximus for the purpose of preserving his hands undefiled, he faithfully adhered to his promise. For after that time he was neither directly nor indirectly concerned in the death of any person, though he sometimes was justly irritated. He swore "that he would perish himself, rather than prove the destruction of any man." Two men of patrician rank being convicted of aspiring to the empire, he only advised them to desist, saying, "that the sovereign power was disposed of by fate," and promised them, that if there was any thing else they desired of him, he would grant it. He also immediately sent messengers to the mother of one of them, who was at a great distance, and in deep anxiety about her son, to assure her of his safety. Nay, he not only invited them to sup with him, but next day, at a show of gladiators, purposely placed them close by him; and handed to them the arms of the combatants for his inspection. It is said likewise, that having had their nativities cast, he assured them, "that a great calamity was impending on both of them, but from another hand, and not from his." Though his brother was continually plotting against him, almost openly stirring up the armies to rebellion, and contriving to get away, yet he could not endure to put him to death, or to banish him from his presence; nor did he treat him with less respect than before. But from his first accession to the empire, he constantly declared him his partner in it, and that he should be his successor; begging of him sometimes in private, with tears in his eyes, "to return the affection he had for him."

X. Amidst all these favourable circumstances, he was cut off by an untimely death, more to the loss of mankind than himself. At the close of the public spectacles, he wept bitterly in the presence of the people, and then retired into the Sabine country , rather melancholy, because a victim had made its escape while he was sacrificing, and loud thunder had been heard while the atmosphere was serene. At the first resting-place on the road, he was seized with a fever, and being carried forward in a litter, they say that he drew back the curtains, and looked up to heaven, complaining heavily, "that his life was taken from him, though he had done nothing to deserve it; for there was no action of his that he had occasion to repent of, but one." What that was, he neither disclosed himself, nor is it easy for us to conjecture. Some imagine that he alluded to the connection which he had formerly had with his brother's wife. But Domitia solemnly denied it on oath; which she would never have done, had there been any truth in the report; nay, she would certainly have gloried in it, as she was forward enough to boast of all her scandalous intrigues.

XI. He died in the same villa where his father had died before him, upon the Ides of September [the 13th of September]; two years, two months, and twenty days after he had succeeded his father; and in the one-and-fortieth year of his age . As soon as the news of his death was published, all people mourned for him, as for the loss of some near relative. The senate assembled in haste, before they could be summoned by proclamation, and locking the doors of their house at first, but afterwards opening them, gave him such thanks, and heaped upon him such praises, now he was dead, as they never had done whilst he was alive and present amongst them.

TITUS FLAVIUS VESPASIAN, the younger, was the first prince who succeeded to the empire by hereditary right; and having constantly acted, after his return from Judaea, as colleague with his father in the administration, he seemed to be as well qualified by experience as he was by abilities, for conducting the affairs of the empire.   But with respect to his natural disposition, and moral behaviour, the expectations entertained by the public were not equally flattering. He was immoderately addicted to luxury; he had betrayed a strong inclination to cruelty; and he lived in the habitual practice of lewdness, no less unnatural than intemperate. But, with a degree of virtuous resolution unexampled in history, he had no sooner taken into his hands the entire reins of government, than he renounced every vicious attachment. Instead of wallowing in luxury, as before, he became a model of temperance; instead of cruelty, he displayed the strongest proofs of humanity and benevolence; and in the room of lewdness, he exhibited a transition to the most unblemished chastity and virtue. In a word, so sudden and great a change was never known in the character of mortal; and he had the peculiar glory to receive the appellation of "the darling and delight of mankind."

Under a prince of such a disposition, the government of the empire could not but be conducted with the strictest regard to the public welfare. The reform, which was begun in the late reign, he prosecuted with the most ardent application; and, had he lived for a longer time, it is probable that his authority and example would have produced the most beneficial effects upon the manners of the Romans.

During the reign of this emperor, in the seventy-ninth year of the Christian era, happened the first eruption of Mount Vesuvius, which has ever since been celebrated for its volcano. Before this time, Vesuvius is spoken of, by ancient writers, as being covered with orchards and vineyards, and of which the middle was dry and barren. The eruption was accompanied by an earthquake, which destroyed several cities of Campania, particularly Pompeii and Herculaneum; while the lava, pouring down the mountain in torrents, overwhelmed, in various directions, the adjacent plains. The burning ashes were carried not only over the neighbouring country, but as far as the shores of Egypt, Libya, and even Syria. Amongst those to whom this dreadful eruption proved fatal, was Pliny, the celebrated naturalist, whose curiosity to examine the phenomenon led him so far within the verge of danger, that he could not afterwards escape.

PLINY, surnamed the Elder, was born at Verona, of a noble family. He distinguished himself early by his military achievements in the German war, received the dignity of an Augur, at Rome, and was afterwards appointed governor of Spain. In every public character, he acquitted himself with great reputation, and enjoyed the esteem of the several emperors under whom he lived. The assiduity with which he applied himself to the collection of information, either curious or useful, surpasses all example. From an early hour in the morning, until late at night, he was almost constantly employed in discharging the duties of his public station, in reading or hearing books read by his amanuensis, and in extracting from them whatever seemed worthy of notice. Even during his meals, and while travelling in his carriage upon business, he prosecuted with unremitting zeal and diligence his taste for enquiry and compilation. No man ever displayed so strong a persuasion of the value of time, or availed himself so industriously of it. He considered every moment as lost which was not employed in literary pursuits. The books which he wrote, in consequence of this indefatigable exertion, were, according to the account transmitted by his nephew, Pliny the younger, numerous, and on various subjects. The catalogue of them is as follows: a book on Equestrian Archery, which discovered much skill in the art; the Life of Q. Pomponius

Secundus; twenty books of the Wars of Germany; a complete treatise on the Education of an Orator, in six volumes; eight books of Doubtful Discourses, written in the latter part of the reign of Nero, when every kind of moral discussion was attended with danger; with a hundred and sixty volumes of remarks on the writings of the various authors which he had perused. For the last-mentioned production only, and before it was brought near to its accomplishment, we are told, that he was offered by Largius Licinius four hundred thousand sesterces, amounting to upwards of three thousand two hundred pounds sterling; an enormous sum for the copyright of a book before the invention of printing! But the only surviving work of this voluminous author is his Natural History, in thirty-seven books, compiled from the various writers who had treated of that extensive and interesting subject.

If we estimate this great work either by the authenticity of the information which it contains, or its utility in promoting the advancement of arts and sciences, we should not consider it as an object of any extraordinary encomiums; but when we view it as a literary monument, which displays the whole knowledge of the ancients, relative to Natural History, collected during a period of about seven hundred years, from the time of Thales the Milesian, it has a just claim to the attention of every speculative enquirer. It is not surprising, that the progress of the human mind, which, in moral science, after the first dawn of enquiry, was rapid both amongst the Greeks and Romans, should be slow in the improvement of such branches of knowledge as depended entirely on observation and facts, which were peculiarly difficult of attainment. Natural knowledge can only be brought to perfection by the prosecution of enquiries in different climates, and by a communication of discoveries amongst those by whom it is cultivated. But neither could enquiries be prosecuted, nor discoveries communicated, with success, while the greater part of the world was involved in barbarism, while navigation was slow and limited, and the art of printing unknown. The consideration of these circumstances will afford sufficient apology for the imperfect state in which natural science existed amongst the ancients. But we proceed to give an abstract of their extent, as they appear in the compilation of Pliny.

This work is divided into thirty-seven books; the first of which contains the Preface, addressed to the emperor Vespasian, probably the father, to whom the author pays high compliments. The second book treats of the world, the elements, and the stars. In respect to the world, or rather the universe, the author's opinion is the same with that of several ancient philosophers, that it is a Deity, uncreated, infinite, and eternal. Their notions, however, as might be expected, on a subject so incomprehensible, are vague, confused, and imperfect. In a subsequent chapter of the same book, where the nature of the Deity is more particularly considered, the author's conceptions of infinite power are so inadequate, that, by way of consolation for the limited powers of man, he observes that there are many things even beyond the power of the Supreme Being; such, for instance, as the annihilation of his own existence; to which the author adds, the power of rendering mortals eternal, and of raising the dead. It deserves to be remarked, that, though a future state of rewards and punishments was maintained by the most eminent among the ancient philosophers, the resurrection of the body was a doctrine with which they were wholly unacquainted.

The author next treats of the planets, and the periods of their respective revolutions; of the stars, comets, winds, thunder, lightning, and other natural phenomena, concerning all which he delivers the hypothetical notions maintained by the ancients, and mentions a variety of extraordinary incidents which had occurred in different parts of the world. The third book contains a general system of geography, which is continued through the fourth, fifth, and sixth books. The seventh treats of conception, and the generation of the human species, with a number of miscellaneous observations, unconnected with the general subject. The eighth treats of quadrupeds; the ninth, of aquatic animals; the tenth, of birds; the eleventh, of insects and reptiles; the twelfth, of trees; the thirteenth, of ointments, and of trees which grow near the sea-coast; the fourteenth, of vines; the fifteenth, of fruit-trees; the sixteenth, of forest-trees; the seventeenth, of the cultivation of trees; the eighteenth, of agriculture; the nineteenth, of the nature of lint, hemp, and similar productions; the twentieth, of the medicinal qualities of vegetables cultivated in gardens; the twenty-first, of flowers; the twenty-second, of the properties of herbs; the twenty-third, of the medicines yielded by cultivated trees; the twenty-fourth, of medicines derived from forest-trees; the twenty-fifth, of the properties of wild herbs, and the origin of their use; the twenty-sixth, of other remedies for diseases, and of some new diseases; the twenty-seventh, of different kinds of herbs; the twenty-eighth, twenty-ninth, and thirtieth, of medicines procured from animals; the thirty-first and thirty-second, of medicines obtained from aquatic animals, with some extraordinary facts relative to the subject; the thirty-third, of the nature of metals; the thirty-fourth, of brass, iron, lead, and tin; the thirty-fifth, of pictures, and observations relative to painting; the thirty-sixth, of the nature of stones and marbles; the thirty-seventh, of the origin of gems. To the contents of each book, the author subjoins a list of the writers from whom his observations have been collected.

Of Pliny's talents as a writer, it might be deemed presumptuous to form a decided opinion from his Natural History, which is avowedly a compilation from various authors, and executed with greater regard to the matter of the work, than to the elegance of composition. Making allowance, however, for a degree of credulity, common to the human mind in the early stage of physical researches, he is far from being deficient in the essential qualifications of a writer of Natural History. His descriptions appear to be accurate, his observations precise, his narrative is in general perspicuous, and he often illustrates his subject by a vivacity of thought, as well as by a happy turn of expression. It has been equally his endeavour to give novelty to stale disquisitions, and authority to new observations. He has both removed the rust, and dispelled the obscurity, which enveloped the doctrines of many ancient naturalists; but, with all his care and industry, he has exploded fewer errors, and sanctioned a greater number of doubtful opinions, than was consistent with the exercise of unprejudiced and severe investigation.

Pliny was fifty-six years of age at the time of his death; the manner of which is accurately related by his nephew, the elegant Pliny the Younger, in a letter to Tacitus, who entertained a design of writing the life of the naturalist.

Titus Flavius Domitianus.

I. Domitian was born upon the ninth of the calends of November [24th October] , when his father was consul elect, (being to enter upon his office the month following,) in the sixth region of the city, at the Pomegranate , in the house which he afterwards converted into a temple of the Flavian family. He is said to have spent the time of his youth in so much want and infamy, that he had not one piece of plate belonging to him; and it is well known, that Clodius Pollio, a man of pretorian rank, against whom there is a poem of Nero's extant, entitled Luscio, kept a note in his hand-writing, which he sometimes produced, in which Domitian made an assignation with him for the foulest purposes. Some, likewise, have said, that he prostituted himself to Nerva, who succeeded him. In the war with Vitellius, he fled into the Capitol with his uncle Sabinus, and a part of the troops they had in the city . But the enemy breaking in, and the temple being set on fire, he hid himself all night with the sacristan; and next morning, assuming the disguise of a worshipper of Isis, and mixing with the priests of that idle superstition, he got over the Tiber , with only one attendant, to the house of a woman who was the mother of one of his school-fellows, and lurked there so close, that, though the enemy, who were at his heels, searched very strictly after him, they could not discover him. At last, after the success of his party, appearing in public, and being unanimously saluted by the title of Caesar, he assumed the office of praetor of the City, with consular authority, but in fact had nothing but the name; for the jurisdiction he transferred to his next colleague. He used, however, his absolute power so licentiously, that even then he plainly discovered what sort of prince he was likely to prove. Not to go into details, after he had made free with the wives of many men of distinction, he took Domitia Longina from her husband, Aelias Lamia, and married her; and in one day disposed of above twenty offices in the city and the provinces; upon which Vespasian said several times, "he wondered he did not send him a successor too."

II. He likewise designed an expedition into Gaul and Germany , without the least necessity for it, and contrary to the advice of all his father's friends; and this he did only with the view of equalling his brother in military achievements and glory. But for this he was severely reprimanded, and that he might the more effectually be reminded of his age and position, was made to live with his father, and his litter had to follow his father's and brother's carriage, as often as they went abroad; but he attended them in their triumph for the conquest of Judaea , mounted on a white horse. Of the six consulships which he held, only one was ordinary; and that he obtained by the cession and interest of his brother. He greatly affected a modest behaviour, and, above all, a taste for poetry; insomuch, that he rehearsed his performances in public, though it was an art he had formerly little cultivated, and which he afterwards despised and abandoned. Devoted, however, as he was at this time to poetical pursuits, yet when Vologesus, king of the Parthians, desired succours against the Alani, with one of Vespasian's sons to command them, he laboured hard to procure for himself that appointment. But the scheme proving abortive, he endeavoured by presents and promises to engage other kings of the East to make a similar request. After his father's death, he was for some time in doubt, whether he should not offer the soldiers a donative double to that of his brother, and made no scruple of saying frequently, "that he had been left his partner in the empire, but that his father's will had been fraudulently set aside." From that time forward, he was constantly engaged in plots against his brother, both publicly and privately; until, falling dangerously ill, he ordered all his attendants to leave him, under pretence of his being dead, before he really was so; and, at his decease, paid him no other honour than that of enrolling him amongst the gods; and he often, both in speeches and edicts, carped at his memory by sneers and insinuations.

III. In the beginning of his reign, he used to spend daily an hour by himself in private, during which time he did nothing else but catch flies, and stick them through the body with a sharp pin. When some one therefore inquired, "whether any one was with the emperor," it was significantly answered by Vibius Crispus, "Not so much as a fly." Soon after his advancement, his wife Domitia, by whom he had a son in his second consulship, and whom the year following he complimented with the title of Augusta, being desperately in love with Paris, the actor, he put her away; but within a short time afterwards, being unable to bear the separation, he took her again, under pretence of complying with the people's importunity. During some time, there was in his administration a strange mixture of virtue and vice, until at last his virtues themselves degenerated into vices; being, as we may reasonably conjecture concerning his character, inclined to avarice through want, and to cruelty through fear.

IV. He frequently entertained the people with most magnificent and costly shows, not only in the amphitheatre, but the circus; where, besides the usual races with chariots drawn by two or four horses a-breast, he exhibited the representation of an engagement between both horse and foot, and a sea-fight in the amphitheatre. The people were also entertained with the chase of wild beasts and the combat of gladiators, even in the night-time, by torch-light. Nor did men only fight in these spectacles, but women also. He constantly attended at the games given by the quaestors, which had been disused for some time, but were revived by him; and upon those occasions, always gave the people the liberty of demanding two pair of gladiators out of his own school, who appeared last in court uniforms. Whenever he attended the shows of gladiators, there stood at his feet a little boy dressed in scarlet, with a prodigiously small head, with whom he used to talk very much, and sometimes seriously. We are assured, that he was overheard asking him, "if he knew for what reason he had in the late appointment, made Metius Rufus governor of Egypt?" He presented the people with naval fights, performed by fleets almost as numerous as those usually employed in real engagements; making a vast lake near the Tiber , and building seats round it. And he witnessed them himself during a very heavy rain. He likewise celebrated the Secular games , reckoning not from the year in which they had been exhibited by Claudius, but from the time of Augustus's celebration of them. In these, upon the day of the Circensian sports, in order to have a hundred races performed, he reduced each course from seven rounds to five. He likewise instituted, in honour of Jupiter Capitolinus, a solemn contest in music to be performed every five years; besides horse-racing and gymnastic exercises, with more prizes than are at present allowed. There was also a public performance in elocution, both Greek and Latin and besides the musicians who sung to the harp, there were others who played concerted pieces or solos, without vocal accompaniment. Young girls also ran races in the Stadium, at which he presided in his sandals, dressed in a purple robe, made after the Grecian fashion, and wearing upon his head a golden crown bearing the effigies of Jupiter, Juno, and Minerva; with the flamen of Jupiter, and the college of priests sitting by his side in the same dress; excepting only that their crowns had also his own image on them. He celebrated also upon the Alban mount every year the festival of Minerva, for whom he had appointed a college of priests, out of which were chosen by lot persons to preside as governors over the college; who were obliged to entertain the people with extraordinary chases of wild-beasts, and stage-plays, besides contests for prizes in oratory and poetry. He thrice bestowed upon the people a largess of three hundred sesterces each man; and, at a public show of gladiators, a very plentiful feast. At the festival of the Seven Hills , he distributed large hampers of provisions to the senatorian and equestrian orders, and small baskets to the common people, and encouraged them to eat by setting them the example. The day after, he scattered among the people a variety of cakes and other delicacies to be scrambled for; and on the greater part of them falling amidst the seats of the crowd, he ordered five hundred tickets to be thrown into each range of benches belonging to the senatorian and equestrian orders.

V. He rebuilt many noble edifices which had been destroyed by fire, and amongst them the Capitol, which had been burnt down a second time ; but all the inscriptions were in his own name, without the least mention of the original founders. He likewise erected a new temple in the Capitol to Jupiter Custos, and a forum, which is now called Nerva's , as also the temple of the Flavian family , a stadium , an odeum , and a naumachia ; out of the stone dug from which, the sides of the Circus Maximus, which had been burnt down, were rebuilt.

VI. He undertook several expeditions, some from choice, and some from necessity. That against the Catti was unprovoked, but that against the Sarmatians was necessary; an entire legion, with its commander, having been cut off by them. He sent two expeditions against the Dacians; the first upon the defeat of Oppius Sabinus, a man of consular rank; and the other, upon that of Cornelius Fuscus, prefect of the pretorian cohorts, to whom he had entrusted the conduct of that war. After several battles with the Catti and Daci, he celebrated a double triumph. But for his successes against the Sarmatians, he only bore in procession the laurel crown to Jupiter Capitolinus. The civil war, begun by Lucius Antonius, governor of Upper Germany, he quelled, without being obliged to be personally present at it, with remarkable good fortune. For, at the very moment of joining battle, the Rhine suddenly thawing, the troops of the barbarians which were ready to join L. Antonius, were prevented from crossing the river. Of this victory he had notice by some presages, before the messengers who brought the news of it arrived. For upon the very day the battle was fought, a splendid eagle spread its wings round his statue at Rome, making most joyful cries. And shortly after, a rumour became common, that Antonius was slain; nay, many positively affirmed, that they saw his head brought to the city.

VII. He made many innovations in common practices. He abolished the Sportula , and revived the old practice of regular suppers. To the four former parties in the Circensian games, he added two new, who were gold and scarlet. He prohibited the players from acting in the theatre, but permitted them the practice of their art in private houses. He forbad the castration of males; and reduced the price of the eunuchs who were still left in the hands of the dealers in slaves. On the occasion of a great abundance of wine, accompanied by a scarcity of corn, supposing that the tillage of the ground was neglected for the sake of attending too much to the cultivation of vineyards, he published a proclamation forbidding the planting of any new vines in Italy, and ordering the vines in the provinces to be cut down, nowhere permitting more than one half of them to remain . But he did not persist in the execution of this project. Some of the greatest offices he conferred upon his freedmen and soldiers. He forbad two legions to be quartered in the same camp, and more than a thousand sesterces to be deposited by any soldier with the standards; because it was thought that Lucius Antonius had been encouraged in his late project by the large sum deposited in the military chest by the two legions which he had in the same winter-quarters. He made an addition to the soldiers' pay, of three gold pieces a year.

VIII. In the administration of justice he was diligent and assiduous; and frequently sat in the Forum out of course, to cancel the judgments of the court of The One Hundred, which had been procured through favour, or interest. He occasionally cautioned the judges of the court of recovery to beware of being too ready to admit claims for freedom brought before them. He set a mark of infamy upon judges who were convicted of taking bribes, as well as upon their assessors. He likewise instigated the tribunes of the people to prosecute a corrupt aedile for extortion, and to desire the senate to appoint judges for his trial. He likewise took such effectual care in punishing magistrates of the city, and governors of provinces, guilty of malversation, that they never were at any time more moderate or more just. Most of these, since his reign, we have seen prosecuted for crimes of various kinds. Having taken upon himself the reformation of the public manners, he restrained the licence of the populace in sitting promiscuously with the knights in the theatre. Scandalous libels, published to defame persons of rank, of either sex, he suppressed, and inflicted upon their authors a mark of infamy. He expelled a man of quaestorian rank from the senate, for practising mimicry and dancing. He debarred infamous women the use of litters; as also the right of receiving legacies, or inheriting estates. He struck out of the list of judges a Roman knight for taking again his wife whom he had divorced and prosecuted for adultery. He condemned several men of the senatorian and equestrian orders, upon the Scantinian law . The lewdness of the Vestal Virgins, which had been overlooked by his father and brother, he punished severely, but in different ways; viz. offences committed before his reign, with death, and those since its commencement, according to ancient custom. For to the two sisters called Ocellatae, he gave liberty to choose the mode of death which they preferred, and banished their paramours. But Cornelia, the president of the Vestals, who had formerly been acquitted upon a charge of incontinence, being a long time after again prosecuted and condemned, he ordered to be buried alive; and her gallants to be whipped to death with rods in the Comitium; excepting only a man of praetorian rank, to whom, because he confessed the fact, while the case was dubious, and it was not established against him, though the witnesses had been put to the torture, he granted the favour of banishment. And to preserve pure and undefiled the reverence due to the gods, he ordered the soldiers to demolish a tomb, which one of his freedmen had erected for his son out of the stones designed for the temple of Jupiter Capitolinus, and to sink in the sea the bones and relics buried in it.

IX. Upon his first succeeding to power, he felt such an abhorrence for the shedding of blood, that, before his father's arrival in Rome, calling to mind the verse of Virgil,

Impia quam caesis gens est epulata juvencis,

Ere impious man, restrain'd from blood in vain,
Began to feast on flesh of bullocks slain,

he designed to have published a proclamation, "to forbid the sacrifice of oxen." Before his accession to the imperial authority, and during some time afterwards, he scarcely ever gave the least grounds for being suspected of covetousness or avarice; but, on the contrary, he often afforded proofs, not only of his justice, but his liberality. To all about him he was generous even to profusion, and recommended nothing more earnestly to them than to avoid doing anything mean. He would not accept the property left him by those who had children. He also set aside a legacy bequeathed by the will of Ruscus Caepio, who had ordered "his heir to make a present yearly to each of the senators upon their first assembling." He exonerated all those who had been under prosecution from the treasury for above five years before; and would not suffer suits to be renewed, unless it was done within a year, and on condition, that the prosecutor should be banished, if he could not make good his cause. The secretaries of the quaestors having engaged in trade, according to custom, but contrary to the Clodian law , he pardoned them for what was past. Such portions of land as had been left when it was divided amongst the veteran soldiers, he granted to the ancient possessors, as belonging to then by prescription. He put a stop to false prosecutions in the exchequer, by severely punishing the prosecutors; and this saying of his was much taken notice of "that a prince who does not punish informers, encourages them."

X. But he did not long persevere in this course of clemency and justice, although he sooner fell into cruelty than into avarice. He put to death a scholar of Paris, the pantomimic , though a minor, and then sick, only because, both in person and the practice of his art, he resembled his master; as he did likewise Hermogenes of Tarsus for some oblique reflections in his History; crucifying, besides, the scribes who had copied the work. One who was master of a band of gladiators, happening to say, "that a Thrax was a match for a Marmillo , but not so for the exhibitor of the games", he ordered him to be dragged from the benches into the arena, and exposed to the dogs, with this label upon him, "A Parmularian guilty of talking impiously." He put to death many senators, and amongst them several men of consular rank. In this number were, Civica Cerealis, when he was proconsul in Africa, Salvidienus Orfitus, and Acilius Glabrio in exile, under the pretence of their planning to revolt against him. The rest he punished upon very trivial occasions; as Aelius Lamia for some jocular expressions, which were of old date, and perfectly harmless; because, upon his commending his voice after he had taken his wife from him , he replied, "Alas! I hold my tongue." And when Titus advised him to take another wife, he answered him thus: "What! have you a mind to marry?" Salvius Cocceianus was condemned to death for keeping the birth-day of his uncle Otho, the emperor: Metius Pomposianus, because he was commonly reported to have an imperial nativity , and to carry about with him a map of the world upon vellum, with the speeches of kings and generals extracted out of Titus Livius; and for giving his slaves the names of Mago and Hannibal; Sallustius Lucullus, lieutenant in Britain, for suffering some lances of a new invention to be called "Lucullean;" and Junius Rusticus, for publishing a treatise in praise of Paetus Thrasea and Helvidius Priscus, and calling them both "most upright men." Upon this occasion, he likewise banished all the philosophers from the city and Italy. He put to death the younger Helvidius, for writing a farce, in which, under the character of Paris and Oenone, he reflected upon his having divorced his wife; and also Flavius Sabinus, one of his cousins, because, upon his being chosen at the consular election to that office, the public crier had, by a blunder, proclaimed him to the people not consul, but emperor. Becoming still more savage after his success in the civil war, he employed the utmost industry to discover those of the adverse party who absconded: many of them he racked with a new-invented torture, inserting fire through their private parts; and from some he cut off their hands. It is certain, that only two of any note were pardoned, a tribune who wore the narrow stripe, and a centurion; who, to clear themselves from the charge of being concerned in any rebellious project, proved themselves to have been guilty of prostitution, and consequently incapable of exercising any influence either over the general or the soldiers.

XI. His cruelties were not only excessive, but subtle and unexpected. The day before he crucified a collector of his rents, he sent for him into his bed-chamber, made him sit down upon the bed by him, and sent him away well pleased, and, so far as could be inferred from his treatment, in a state of perfect security; having vouchsafed him the favour of a plate of meat from his own table. When he was on the point of condemning to death Aretinus Clemens, a man of consular rank, and one of his friends and emissaries, he retained him about his person in the same or greater favour than ever; until at last, as they were riding together in the same litter, upon seeing the man who had informed against him, he said, "Are you willing that we should hear this base slave tomorrow?" Contemptuously abusing the patience of men, he never pronounced a severe sentence without prefacing it with words which gave hopes of mercy; so that, at last, there was not a more certain token of a fatal conclusion, than a mild commencement. He brought before the senate some persona accused of treason, declaring, "that he should prove that day how dear he was to the senate;" and so influenced them, that they condemned the accused to be punished according to the ancient usage . Then, as if alarmed at the extreme severity of their punishment, to lessen the odiousness of the proceeding, he interposed in these words; for it is not foreign to the purpose to give them precisely as they were delivered: "Permit me, Conscript Fathers, so far to prevail upon your affection for me, however extraordinary the request may seem, as to grant the condemned criminals the favour of dying in the manner they choose. For by so doing, ye will spare your own eyes, and the world will understand that I interceded with the senate on their behalf."

XII. Having exhausted the exchequer by the expense of his buildings and public spectacles, with the augmentation of pay lately granted to the troops, he made an attempt at the reduction of the army, in order to lessen the military charges. But reflecting, that he should, by this measure, expose himself to the insults of the barbarians, while it would not suffice to extricate him from his embarrassments, he had recourse to plundering his subjects by every mode of exaction. The estates of the living and the dead were sequestered upon any accusation, by whomsoever preferred. The unsupported allegation of any one person, relative to a word or action construed to affect the dignity of the emperor, was sufficient. Inheritances, to which he had not the slightest pretension, were confiscated, if there was found so much as one person to say, he had heard from the deceased when living, "that he had made the emperor his heir." Besides the exactions from others, the poll-tax on the Jews was levied with extreme rigour, both on those who lived after the manner of Jews in the city, without publicly professing themselves to be such , and on those who, by concealing their origin, avoided paying the tribute imposed upon that people. I remember, when I was a youth, to have been present , when an old man, ninety years of age, had his person exposed to view in a very crowded court, in order that, on inspection, the procurator might satisfy himself whether he was circumcised.

From his earliest years Domitian was any thing but courteous, of a forward, assuming disposition, and extravagant both in his words and actions. When Caenis, his father's concubine, upon her return from Istria, offered him a kiss, as she had been used to do, he presented her his hand to kiss. Being indignant, that his brother's son-in-law should be waited on by servants dressed in white , he exclaimed,

ouk agathon polykoiraniae.
Too many princes are not good.

XIII. After he became emperor, he had the assurance to boast in the senate, "that he had bestowed the empire on his father and brother, and they had restored it to him." And upon taking his wife again, after the divorce, he declared by proclamation, "that he had recalled her to his pulvinar." He was not a little pleased too, at hearing the acclamations of the people in the amphitheatre on a day of festival, "All happiness to our lord and lady." But when, during the celebration of the Capitoline trial of skill, the whole concourse of people entreated him with one voice to restore Palfurius Sura to his place in the senate, from which he had been long before expelled—he having then carried away the prize of eloquence from all the orators who had contended for it,—he did not vouchsafe to give them any answer, but only commanded silence to be proclaimed by the voice of the crier. With equal arrogance, when he dictated the form of a letter to be used by his procurators, he began it thus: "Our lord and god commands so and so;" whence it became a rule that no one should style him otherwise either in writing or speaking. He suffered no statues to be erected for him in the Capitol, unless they were of gold and silver, and of a certain weight. He erected so many magnificent gates and arches, surmounted by representations of chariots drawn by four horses, and other triumphal ornaments, in different quarters of the city, that a wag inscribed on one of the arches the Greek word Axkei, "It is enough." He filled the office of consul seventeen times, which no one had ever done before him, and for the seven middle occasions in successive years; but in scarcely any of them had he more than the title; for he never continued in office beyond the calends of May [the 1st May], and for the most part only till the ides of January [13th January]. After his two triumphs, when he assumed the cognomen of Germanicus, he called the months of September and October, Germanicus and Domitian, after his own names, because he commenced his reign in the one, and was born in the other.

XIV. Becoming by these means universally feared and odious, he was at last taken off by a conspiracy of his friends and favourite freedmen, in concert with his wife . He had long entertained a suspicion of the year and day when he should die, and even of the very hour and manner of his death; all which he had learned from the Chaldaeans, when he was a very young man. His father once at supper laughed at him for refusing to eat some mushrooms, saying, that if he knew his fate, he would rather be afraid of the sword. Being, therefore, in perpetual apprehension and anxiety, he was keenly alive to the slightest suspicions, insomuch that he is thought to have withdrawn the edict ordering the destruction of the vines, chiefly because the copies of it which were dispersed had the following lines written upon them:

Kaen me phagaes epi rizanomos epi kartophoraeso,
    Osson epispeisai Kaisari thuomeno.

Gnaw thou my root, yet shall my juice suffice
To pour on Caesar's head in sacrifice.

It was from the same principle of fear, that he refused a new honour, devised and offered him by the senate, though he was greedy of all such compliments. It was this: "that as often as he held the consulship, Roman knights, chosen by lot, should walk before him, clad in the Trabea, with lances in their hands, amongst his lictors and apparitors." As the time of the danger which he apprehended drew near, he became daily more and more disturbed in mind; insomuch that he lined the walls of the porticos in which he used to walk, with the stone called Phengites , by the reflection of which he could see every object behind him. He seldom gave an audience to persons in custody, unless in private, being alone, and he himself holding their chains in his hand. To convince his domestics that the life of a master was not to be attempted upon any pretext, however plausible, he condemned to death Epaphroditus his secretary, because it was believed that he had assisted Nero, in his extremity, to kill himself.

XV. His last victim was Flavius Clemens , his cousin-german, a man below contempt for his want of energy, whose sons, then of very tender age, he had avowedly destined for his successors, and, discarding their former names, had ordered one to be called Vespasian, and the other Domitian. Nevertheless, he suddenly put him to death upon some very slight suspicion , almost before he was well out of his consulship. By this violent act he very much hastened his own destruction. During eight months together there was so much lightning at Rome, and such accounts of the phaenomenon were brought from other parts, that at last he cried out, "Let him now strike whom he will." The Capitol was struck by lightning, as well as the temple of the Flavian family, with the Palatine-house, and his own bed-chamber. The tablet also, inscribed upon the base of his triumphal statue was carried away by the violence of the storm, and fell upon a neighbouring monument. The tree which just before the advancement of Vespasian had been prostrated, and rose again , suddenly fell to the ground. The goddess Fortune of Praeneste, to whom it was his custom on new year's day to commend the empire for the ensuing year, and who had always given him a favourable reply, at last returned him a melancholy answer, not without mention of blood. He dreamt that Minerva, whom he worshipped even to a superstitious excess, was withdrawing from her sanctuary, declaring she could protect him no longer, because she was disarmed by Jupiter. Nothing, however, so much affected him as an answer given by Ascletario, the astrologer, and his subsequent fate. This person had been informed against, and did not deny his having predicted some future events, of which, from the principles of his art, he confessed he had a foreknowledge. Domitian asked him, what end he thought he should come to himself? To which replying, "I shall in a short time be torn to pieces by dogs," he ordered him immediately to be slain, and, in order to demonstrate the vanity of his art, to be carefully buried. But during the preparations for executing this order, it happened that the funeral pile was blown down by a sudden storm, and the body, half-burnt, was torn to pieces by dogs; which being observed by Latinus, the comic actor, as he chanced to pass that way, he told it, amongst the other news of the day, to the emperor at supper.

XVI. The day before his death, he ordered some dates , served up at table, to be kept till the next day, adding, "If I have the luck to use them." And turning to those who were nearest him, he said, "To-morrow the moon in Aquarius will be bloody instead of watery, and an event will happen, which will be much talked of all the world over." About midnight, he was so terrified that he leaped out of bed. That morning he tried and passed sentence on a soothsayer sent from Germany, who being consulted about the lightning that had lately happened, predicted from it a change of government. The blood running down his face as he scratched an ulcerous tumour on his forehead, he said, "Would this were all that is to befall me!" Then, upon his asking the time of the day, instead of five o'clock, which was the hour he dreaded, they purposely told him it was six. Overjoyed at this information; as if all danger were now passed, and hastening to the bath, Parthenius, his chamberlain, stopped him, by saying that there was a person come to wait upon him about a matter of great importance, which would admit of no delay. Upon this, ordering all persons to withdraw, he retired into his chamber, and was there slain.

XVII. Concerning the contrivance and mode of his death, the common account is this. The conspirators being in some doubt when and where they should attack him, whether while he was in the bath, or at supper, Stephanus, a steward of Domitilla's , then under prosecution for defrauding his mistress, offered them his advice and assistance; and wrapping up his left arm, as if it was hurt, in wool and bandages for some days, to prevent suspicion, at the hour appointed, he secreted a dagger in them. Pretending then to make a discovery of a conspiracy, and being for that reason admitted, he presented to the emperor a memorial, and while he was reading it in great astonishment, stabbed him in the groin. But Domitian, though wounded, making resistance, Clodianus, one of his guards, Maximus, a freedman of Parthenius's, Saturius, his principal chamberlain, with some gladiators, fell upon him, and stabbed him in seven places. A boy who had the charge of the Lares in his bed-chamber, and was then in attendance as usual, gave these further particulars: that he was ordered by Domitian, upon receiving his first wound, to reach him a dagger which lay under his pillow, and call in his domestics; but that he found nothing at the head of the bed, excepting the hilt of a poniard, and that all the doors were fastened: that the emperor in the mean time got hold of Stephanus, and throwing him upon the ground, struggled a long time with him; one while endeavouring to wrench the dagger from him, another while, though his fingers were miserably mangled, to tear out his eyes. He was slain upon the fourteenth of the calends of October [18th Sept.], in the forty-fifth year of his age, and the fifteenth of his reign . His corpse was carried out upon a common bier by the public bearers, and buried by his nurse Phyllis, at his suburban villa on the Latin Way. But she afterwards privately conveyed his remains to the temple of the Flavian family , and mingled them with the ashes of Julia, the daughter of Titus, whom she had also nursed.

XVIII. He was tall in stature, his face modest, and very ruddy; he had large eyes, but was dim-sighted; naturally graceful in his person, particularly in his youth, excepting only that his toes were bent somewhat inward, he was at last disfigured by baldness, corpulence, and the slenderness of his legs, which were reduced by a long illness. He was so sensible how much the modesty of his countenance recommended him, that he once made this boast to the senate, "Thus far you have approved both of my disposition and my countenance." His baldness so much annoyed him, that he considered it an affront to himself, if any other person was reproached with it, either in jest or in earnest; though in a small tract he published, addressed to a friend, "concerning the preservation of the hair," he uses for their mutual consolation the words following:

Ouch oraas oios kago kalos te megas te;
Seest thou my graceful mien, my stately form?

"and yet the fate of my hair awaits me; however, I bear with fortitude this loss of my hair while I am still young. Remember that nothing is more fascinating than beauty, but nothing of shorter duration."

XIX. He so shrunk from undergoing fatigue, that he scarcely ever walked through the city on foot. In his expeditions and on a march, he seldom rode on horse-back; but was generally carried in a litter. He had no inclination for the exercise of arms, but was very expert in the use of the bow. Many persons have seen him often kill a hundred wild animals, of various kinds, at his Alban retreat, and fix his arrows in their heads with such dexterity, that he could, in two shots, plant them, like a pair of horns, in each. He would sometimes direct his arrows against the hand of a boy standing at a distance, and expanded as a mark, with such precision, that they all passed between the boy's fingers, without hurting him.

XX. In the beginning of his reign, he gave up the study of the liberal sciences, though he took care to restore, at a vast expense, the libraries which had been burnt down; collecting manuscripts from all parts, and sending scribes to Alexandria , either to copy or correct them. Yet he never gave himself the trouble of reading history or poetry, or of employing his pen even for his private purposes. He perused nothing but the Commentaries and Acts of Tiberius Caesar. His letters, speeches, and edicts, were all drawn up for him by others; though he could converse with elegance, and sometimes expressed himself in memorable sentiments. "I could wish," said he once, "that I was but as handsome as Metius fancies himself to be." And of the head of some one whose hair was partly reddish, and partly grey, he said, "that it was snow sprinkled with mead."

XXI. "The lot of princes," he remarked, "was very miserable, for no one believed them when they discovered a conspiracy, until they were murdered." When he had leisure, he amused himself with dice, even on days that were not festivals, and in the morning. He went to the bath early, and made a plentiful dinner, insomuch that he seldom ate more at supper than a Matian apple , to which he added a draught of wine, out of a small flask. He gave frequent and splendid entertainments, but they were soon over, for he never prolonged them after sun-set, and indulged in no revel after. For, till bed-time, he did nothing else but walk by himself in private.

XXII. He was insatiable in his lusts, calling frequent commerce with women, as if it was a sort of exercise, klinopalaen, bed-wrestling; and it was reported that he plucked the hair from his concubines, and swam about in company with the lowest prostitutes. His brother's daughter was offered him in marriage when she was a virgin; but being at that time enamoured of Domitia, he obstinately refused her. Yet not long afterwards, when she was given to another, he was ready enough to debauch her, and that even while Titus was living. But after she had lost both her father and her husband, he loved her most passionately, and without disguise; insomuch that he was the occasion of her death, by obliging her to procure a miscarriage when she was with child by him.

XXIII. The people shewed little concern at his death, but the soldiers were roused by it to great indignation, and immediately endeavoured to have him ranked among the gods. They were also ready to revenge his loss, if there had been any to take the lead. However, they soon after effected it, by resolutely demanding the punishment of all those who had been concerned in his assassination. On the other hand, the senate was so overjoyed, that they met in all haste, and in a full assembly reviled his memory in the most bitter terms; ordering ladders to be brought in, and his shields and images to be pulled down before their eyes, and dashed in pieces upon the floor of the senate-house passing at the same time a decree to obliterate his titles every where, and abolish all memory of him. A few months before he was slain, a raven on the Capitol uttered these words: "All will be well." Some person gave the following interpretation of this prodigy:

Nuper Tarpeio quae sedit culmine cornix.
"Est bene," non potuit dicere; dixit, "Erit."

Late croaked a raven from Tarpeia's height,
"All is not yet, but shall be, right."

They say likewise that Domitian dreamed that a golden hump grew out of the back of his neck, which he considered as a certain sign of happy days for the empire after him. Such an auspicious change indeed shortly afterwards took place, through the justice and moderation of the succeeding emperors.

If we view Domitian in the different lights in which he is represented, during his lifetime and after his decease, his character and conduct discover a greater diversity than is commonly observed in the objects of historical detail. But as posthumous character is always the most just, its decisive verdict affords the surest criterion by which this variegated emperor must be estimated by impartial posterity. According to this rule, it is beyond a doubt that his vices were more predominant than his virtues: and when we follow him into his closet, for some time after his accession, when he was thirty years of age, the frivolity of his daily employment, in the killing of flies, exhibits an instance of dissipation, which surpasses all that has been recorded of his imperial predecessors. The encouragement, however, which the first Vespasian had shown to literature, continued to operate during the present reign; and we behold the first fruits of its auspicious influence in the valuable treatise of QUINTILIAN.

Of the life of this celebrated writer, little is known upon any authority that has a title to much credit. We learn, however, that he was the son of a lawyer in the service of some of the preceding emperors, and was born in Rome, though in what consulship, or under what emperor, it is impossible to determine. He married a woman of a noble family, by whom he had two sons. The mother died in the flower of her age, and the sons, at the distance of some time from each other, when their father was advanced in years. The precise time of Quintilian's own death is equally inauthenticated with that of his birth; nor can we rely upon an author of suspicious veracity, who says that he passed the latter part of his life in a state of indigence which was alleviated by the liberality of his pupil, Pliny the Younger. Quintilian opened a school of rhetoric at Rome, where he not only discharged that labourious employment with great applause, during more than twenty years, but pleaded at the bar, and was the first who obtained a salary from the state, for executing the office of a public teacher. He was also appointed by Domitian preceptor to the two young princes who were intended to succeed him on the throne.

After his retirement from the situation of a teacher, Quintilian devoted his attention to the study of literature, and composed a treatise on the Causes of the Corruption of Eloquence. At the earnest solicitation of his friends, he was afterwards induced to undertake his Institutiones Oratoriae, the most elaborate system of oratory extant in any language. This work is divided into twelve books, in which the author treats with great precision of the qualities of a perfect orator; explaining not only the fundamental principles of eloquence, as connected with the constitution of the human mind, but pointing out, both by argument and observation, the most successful method of exercising that admirable art, for the accomplishment of its purpose. So minutely, and upon so extensive a plan, has he prosecuted the subject, that he delineates the education suitable to a perfect orator, from the stage of infancy in the cradle, to the consummation of rhetorical fame, in the pursuits of the bar, or those, in general, of any public assembly. It is sufficient to say, that in the execution of this elaborate work, Quintilian has called to the assistance of his own acute and comprehensive understanding, the profound penetration of Aristotle, the exquisite graces of Cicero; all the stores of observation, experience, and practice; and in a word, the whole accumulated exertions of ancient genius on the subject of oratory.

It may justly be regarded as an extraordinary circumstance in the progress of scientific improvement, that the endowments of a perfect orator were never fully exhibited to the world, until it had become dangerous to exercise them for the important purposes for which they were originally cultivated. And it is no less remarkable, that, under all the violence and caprice of imperial despotism which the Romans had now experienced, their sensibility to the enjoyment of poetical compositions remained still unabated; as if it served to console the nation for the irretrievable loss of public liberty. From this source of entertainment, they reaped more pleasure during the present reign, than they had done since the time of Augustus. The poets of this period were Juvenal, Statius, and Martial.

JUVENAL was born at Aquinum, but in what year is uncertain; though, from some circumstances, it seems to have been in the reign of Augustus. Some say that he was the son of a freedman, while others, without specifying the condition of his father, relate only that he was brought up by a freedman. He came at an early age to Rome, where he declaimed for many years, and, pleaded causes in the forum with great applause; but at last he betook himself to the writing of satires, in which he acquired great fame. One of the first, and the most constant object of is satire, was the pantomime Paris, the great favourite of the emperor Nero, and afterwards of Domitian. During the reign of the former of these emperors, no resentment was shown towards the poet; but he experienced not the same impunity after the accession of the latter; when, to remove him from the capital, he was sent as governor to the frontiers of Egypt, but in reality, into an honourable exile. According to some authors, he died of chagrin in that province: but this is not authenticated, and seems to be a mistake: for in some of Martial's epigrams, which appear to have been written after the death of Domitian, Juvenal is spoken of as residing at Rome. It is said that he lived to upwards of eighty years of age.

The remaining compositions of this author are sixteen satires, all written against the dissipation and enormous vices which prevailed at Rome in his time. The various objects of animadversion are painted in the strongest colours, and placed in the most conspicuous points of view. Giving loose reins to just and moral indignation, Juvenal is every where animated, vehement, petulant, and incessantly acrimonious. Disdaining the more lenient modes of correction, or despairing of their success, he neither adopts the raillery of Horace, nor the derision of Persius, but prosecutes vice and folly with all the severity of sentiment, passion, and expression. He sometimes exhibits a mixture of humour with his invectives; but it is a humour which partakes more of virulent rage than of pleasantry; broad, hostile, but coarse, and rivalling in indelicacy the profligate manners which it assails. The satires of Juvenal abound in philosophical apophthegms; and, where they are not sullied by obscene description, are supported with a uniform air of virtuous elevation. Amidst all the intemperance of sarcasm, his numbers are harmonious. Had his zeal permitted him to direct the current of his impetuous genius into the channel of ridicule, and endeavour to put to shame the vices and follies of those licentious times, as much as he perhaps exasperated conviction rather than excited contrition, he would have carried satire to the highest possible pitch, both of literary excellence and moral utility. With every abatement of attainable perfection, we hesitate not to place him at the head of this arduous department of poetry.

Of STATIUS no farther particulars are preserved than that he was born at Naples; that his father's name was Statius of Epirus, and his mother's Agelina, and that he died about the end of the first century of the Christian era. Some have conjectured that he maintained himself by writing for the stage, but of this there is no sufficient evidence; and if ever he composed dramatic productions, they have perished. The works of Statius now extant, are two poems, viz. the Thebais and the Achilleis, besides a collection, named Silvae.

The Thebais consists of twelve books, and the subject of it is the Theban war, which happened 1236 years before the Christian era, in consequence of a dispute between Eteocles and Polynices, the sons of Oedipus and Jocasta. These brothers had entered into an agreement with each other to reign alternately for a year at a time; and Eteocles being the elder, got first possession of the throne. This prince refusing to abdicate at the expiration of the year, Polynices fled to Argos, where marrying Argia, the daughter of Adrastus, king of that country, he procured the assistance of his father-in-law, to enforce the engagement stipulated with his brother Eteocles. The Argives marched under the command of seven able generals, who were to attack separately the seven gates of Thebes. After much blood had been spilt without any effect, it was at last agreed between the two parties, that the brothers should determine the dispute by single combat. In the desperate engagement which ensued, they both fell; and being burnt together upon the funeral pile, it is said that their ashes separated, as if actuated by the implacable resentment which they had borne to each other.

If we except the Aeneid, this is the only Latin production extant which is epic in its form; and it likewise approaches nearest in merit to that celebrated poem, which Statius appears to have been ambitious of emulating. In unity and greatness of action, the Thebais corresponds to the laws of the Epopea; but the fable may be regarded as defective in some particulars, which, however, arise more from the nature of the subject, than from any fault of the poet. The distinction of the hero is not sufficiently prominent; and the poem possesses not those circumstances which are requisite towards interesting the reader's affections in the issue of the contest. To this it may be added, that the unnatural complexion of the incestuous progeny diffuses a kind of gloom which obscures the splendour of thought, and restrains the sympathetic indulgence of fancy to some of the boldest excursions of the poet. For grandeur, however, and animation of sentiment and description, as well as for harmony of numbers, the Thebais is eminently conspicuous, and deserves to be held in a much higher degree of estimation than it has generally obtained. In the contrivance of some of the episodes, and frequently in the modes of expression, Statius keeps an attentive eye to the style of Virgil. It is said that he was twelve years employed in the composition of this poem; and we have his own authority for affirming, that he polished it with all the care and assiduity practised by the poets in the Augustan age:

Quippe, te fido monitore, nostra
Thebais, multa cruciata lima,
Tentat audaci fide Mantuanae
    Gaudia famae.—Silvae, lib. iv. 7.

For, taught by you, with steadfast care
I trim my "Song of Thebes," and dare
With generous rivalry to share
    The glories of the Mantuan bard.

The Achilleis relates to the same hero who is celebrated by Homer in the Iliad; but it is the previous history of Achilles, not his conduct in the Trojan war, which forms the subject of the poem of Statius. While the young hero is under the care of the Centaur Chiron, Thetis makes a visit to the preceptor's sequestered habitation, where, to save her son from the fate which, it was predicted, would befall him at Troy, if he should go to the siege of that place, she orders him to be dressed in the disguise of a girl, and sent to live in the family of Lycomedes, king of Scyros. But as Troy could not be taken without the aid of Achilles, Ulysses, accompanied by Diomede, is deputed by the Greeks to go to Scyros, and bring him thence to the Grecian camp. The artifice by which the sagacious ambassador detected Achilles amongst his female companions, was by placing before them various articles of merchandise, amongst which was some armour. Achilles no sooner perceived the latter, than he eagerly seized a sword and shield, and manifesting the strongest emotions of heroic enthusiasm, discovered his sex. After an affectionate parting with Lycomedes' daughter, Deidamia, whom he left pregnant of a son, he set sail with the Grecian chiefs, and, during the voyage, gives them an account of the manner of his education with Chiron.

This poem consists of two books, in heroic measure, and is written with taste and fancy. Commentators are of opinion, that the Achilleis was left incomplete by the death of the author; but this is extremely improbable, from various circumstances, and appears to be founded only upon the word Hactenus, in the conclusion of the poem:

> Hactenus annorum, comites, elementa meorum
> Et memini, et meminisse juvat: scit caetera mater.

> Thus far, companions dear, with mindful joy I've told
> My youthful deeds; the rest my mother can unfold.

That any consequential reference was intended by hactenus, seems to me plainly contradicted by the words which immediately follow, scit caetera mater. Statius could not propose the giving any further account of Achilles's life, because a general narrative of it had been given in the first book. The voyage from Scyros to the Trojan coast, conducted with the celerity which suited the purpose of the poet, admitted of no incidents which required description or recital: and after the voyagers had reached the Grecian camp, it is reasonable to suppose, that the action of the Iliad immediately commenced. But that Statius had no design of extending the plan of the Achilleis beyond this period, is expressly declared in the exordium of the poem:

> Magnanimum Aeaciden, formidatamque Tonanti
> Progeniem, et patrio vetitam succedere coelo,
> Diva, refer; quanquam acta viri multum inclyta cantu
> Maeonio; sed plura vacant. Nos ire per omnem
> (Sic amor est) heroa velis, Scyroque latentem
> Dulichia proferre tuba: nec in Hectore tracto
> Sistere, sed tota juvenem deducere Troja.

> Aid me, O goddess! while I sing of him,
> Who shook the Thunderer's throne, and, for his crime,
> Was doomed to lose his birthright in the skies;
> The great Aeacides. Maeonian strains
> Have made his mighty deeds their glorious theme;
> Still much remains: be mine the pleasing task
> To trace the future hero's young career,
> Not dragging Hector at his chariot wheels,
> But while disguised in Scyros yet he lurked,

Till trumpet-stirred, he sprung to manly arms,
And sage Ulysses led him to the Trojan coast.

The Silvae is a collection of poems almost entirely in heroic verse, divided into five books, and for the most part written extempore. Statius himself affirms, in his Dedication to Stella, that the production of none of them employed him more than two days; yet many of them consist of between one hundred and two hundred hexameter lines. We meet with one of two hundred and sixteen lines; one, of two hundred and thirty-four; one, of two hundred and sixty-two; and one of two hundred and seventy-seven; a rapidity of composition approaching to what Horace mentions of the poet Lucilius. It is no small encomium to observe, that, considered as extemporaneous productions, the meanest in the collection is far from meriting censure, either in point of sentiment or expression; and many of them contain passages which command our applause.

The poet MARTIAL, surnamed likewise Coquus, was born at Bilbilis, in Spain, of obscure parents. At the age of twenty-one, he came to Rome, where he lived during five-and-thirty years under the emperors Galba, Otho, Vitellius, the two Vespasians, Domitian, Nerva, and the beginning of the reign of Trajan. He was the panegyrist of several of those emperors, by whom he was liberally rewarded, raised to the Equestrian order, and promoted by Domitian to the tribuneship; but being treated with coldness and neglect by Trajan, he returned to his native country, and, a few years after, ended his days, at the age of seventy-five.

He had lived at Rome in great splendour and affluence, as well as in high esteem for his poetical talents; but upon his return to Bilbilis, it is said that he experienced a great reverse of fortune, and was chiefly indebted for his support to the gratuitous benefactions of Pliny the Younger, whom he had extolled in some epigrams.

The poems of Martial consist of fourteen books, all written in the epigrammatic form, to which species of composition, introduced by the Greeks, he had a peculiar propensity. Amidst such a multitude of verses, on a variety of subjects, often composed extempore, and many of them, probably, in the moments of fashionable dissipation, it is not surprising that we find a large number unworthy the genius of the author. Delicacy, and even decency, is often violated in the productions of Martial. Grasping at every thought which afforded even the shadow of ingenuity, he gave unlimited scope to the exercise of an active and fruitful imagination. In respect to composition, he is likewise liable to censure. At one time he wearies, and at another tantalises the reader, with the prolixity or ambiguity of his preambles. His prelusive sentiments are sometimes far-fetched, and converge not with a natural declination into the focus of epigram. In dispensing praise and censure, he often seems to be governed more by prejudice or policy, than by justice and truth; and he is more constantly attentive to the production of wit, than to the improvement of morality.

But while we remark the blemishes and imperfections of this poet, we must acknowledge his extraordinary merits. In composition he is, in general, elegant and correct; and where the subject is capable of connection with sentiment, his inventive ingenuity never fails to extract from it the essence of delight and surprise. His fancy is prolific of beautiful images, and his judgment expert in arranging them to the greatest advantage. He bestows panegyric with inimitable grace, and satirises with equal dexterity. In a fund of Attic salt, he surpasses every other writer; and though he seems to have at command all the varied stores of gall, he is not destitute of candour. With almost every kind of versification he appears to be familiar; and notwithstanding a facility of temper, too accommodating, perhaps, on many occasions, to the licentiousness of the times, we may venture from strong indications to pronounce, that, as a moralist, his principles were virtuous. It is observed of this author, by Pliny the Younger, that, though his compositions might, perhaps, not obtain immortality, he wrote as if they would. [Aeterna, quae scripsit, non erunt fortasse: ille tamen scripsit tanquam futura.] The character which Martial gives of his epigrams, is just and comprehensive:

Sunt bona, sunt quaedam mediocria, sunt mala plura,
Quae legis: hic aliter non fit, Avite, liber.

Some are good, some indifferent, and some again still worse;
Such, Avitus, you will find is a common case with verse.

Lightning Source UK Ltd.
Milton Keynes UK
UKHW01f1958110618
324081UK00001B/144/P